Contents

A leap and a bite

A large shark sees a seal

near the ocean's surface.

Zoom! The shark races upwards.

It leaps into the air

and catches the seal.

Great white sharks are the largest hunting fish in the world. They live in mostly cool seas.

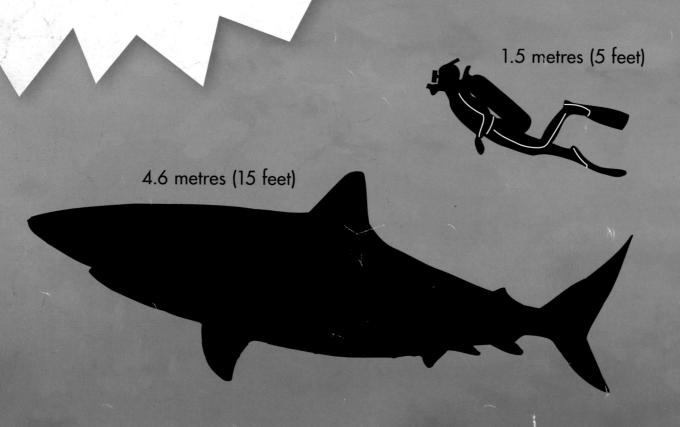

1.5 metres (5 feet)

4.6 metres (15 feet)

A rugby ball-shaped fish

A great white's body
looks like a long rugby ball.
This shape helps the shark
speed through the water.

9

A great white shark is
not all white. It has a grey
back and a white belly.
The grey colour blends in
with the ocean floor.

Great whites have a nostril on each side of their snout. They use their nostrils to smell prey. Great whites can smell blood from far away.

nostrils

Hunting and eating

Great white sharks hunt seals,
sea lions and small whales.
A big meal can feed one of these
sharks for more than a month.

A great white shark's jaws

hold about 300 sharp teeth.

Few animals can escape

its jaws.

Great white babies

Great white shark pups are born live. Between 2 and 10 pups are born at one time. The pups are about 1.5 metres (5 feet) long.

19

The pups leave their mother straight away. Young great whites live on their own. These sharks can live for more than 30 years.

Glossary

escape get away from

hunt find and catch animals for food

nostril one of the two outside openings in the nose used to breathe and smell

prey animal hunted by another animal for food

pup young shark

snout long front part of an animal's head; it includes the nose, mouth and jaws

surface outside or outermost area of something

Find out more

Books

DK Findout! Sharks, DK (DK Publishing, 2017)

Killer Whale vs. Great White Shark (Who Would Win?), Jerry Pallotta (Scholastic, 2015)

Sharks for Kids, Awesome Earth for Kids (Awesome Earth, 2013) Waxman, Laura Hamilton.

Websites

www.bbc.co.uk/programmes/p02n7s0d/clips
Watch lots of amazing videos of sharks in action at this BBC website.

www.ducksters.com/animals/greatwhiteshark.php
Learn more fun facts about great white sharks at this website.

Comprehension questions

1. How do great white sharks catch seals?

2. What does a great white shark look like?

3. What is a nostril? How does a great white shark's nostrils help it to catch prey?

Index